MW00903217

FRIDAY MEMORIES

The Life and Times of

June Friday MacInnis

FriesenPress

Suite 300 - 990 Fort St

Victoria, BC, V8V 3K2

Canada

www.friesenpress.com

ISBN

978-1-4602-8405-6 (Hardcover)

978-1-4602-8406-3 (Paperback)

978-1-4602-8407-0 (eBook)

1. HISTORY, SOCIAL HISTORY

Distributed to the trade by The Ingram Book Company

This book is in memory of my daughter Melissa,
who is waiting for me with our Creator.

I also dedicate this book to my dear friend Marie-Claude
who encouraged me and gave me the con-
fidence to publish these stories.

Table of Contents

Foreword

My six granddaughters, at ages six and up, were always asking: "How did Grandpa and Grandma get to Temagami? How was Friday's Camp started? What did you do when you were a little girl? Where did you go to school? Did your mom or dad ever live in teepees?" So many questions!

So one day, I thought I'd write about where my father came from, because he and my uncle told me about where they had lived and how my grandfather had worked for the Hudson's Bay Company. That's how these memories got started. I want my grandchildren and their descendants to know how resourceful and generous their ancestors were, and how they we able to thrive despite the difficulties.

I also hope that others will be inspired to share their stories so that they are not lost as our Elders pass on.

June Friday MacInnis

Part 1
Family History

There were four brothers whose names were Matthew, Mark, Luke and John. The Jesuit missionaries gave them these names. John chose the last name to be Friday. The other brothers kept their first names as their last names. So we are related to the Matthews, Marks and Lukes from the James Bay area.

John Friday married Margaret Sanders who was born on October 4, 1842 at Flying Post (Northwestern Ontario). Her brother was Rev. John Sanders, who was the first Native missionary and who transcribed the Bible into Cree. They moved to Fort Matagami at a Hudson Bay Post where John Friday was employed. *Koomsubiin* (Grandmother Margaret Sanders) told my mother (Sophie Potts) about going for cedar brush for beds and brooms, and having to be careful because Iroquois war parties were roaming and were kidnapping young girls and women for mates.

John and Margaret had Tom, Jim, Ellen, George, the twins Joe and Charlotte, and Willie. The family paddled down the Montreal River, heading to Temagami. On the way down, John's canoe upset and he became sick with pneumonia and died. When they reached Temagami, they met with some missionaries who gave him a Christian burial. His grave is at Bear Island Anglican graveyard.

At Temagami, the family was adopted by the chief, who was White Bear at the time. They lived in Petrant's barn until Jim Friday found a suitable ground to build on. This is what became known as 'Friday's Point', *Naadgaaming*, across the lake. There, Jim built a log cabin for the family.

And as my dad, Willie Friday told me, when the cabin had the roof, walls and floor, but no doors or windows yet, some tourists came paddling by and asked if they could rent it as it was. Of course he said "yes." So this gave my dad the idea for a tourist camp, and he continued to guide, trap and save for his dream.

Jim Friday, Phil, Charley and Old Jim at Sagmaster's Island on Jackpine Lake

Jim Friday with Mr. and Mrs. Sagmaster

Jim, the oldest, was the farmer. So he planted a garden of root vegetables first and as time went by, they had a cow, pigs, a horse and a donkey. Jim's potatoes were his best, and he sold them to the camps around the lake and also to surveyors' camps when the highway and railway were going north.

The young men from Bear Island would help plant and harvest the crops. And for payment, he would give each helper a 75-pound bag of potatoes. Jim never married and lived at Friday's Point with his mother, and his brothers and sisters.

Willie Friday and Old Jim at camp

The girls… Ellen Friday married Joe Turner, Charlotte married Fred Potts and George married Mary Beaucage. The marriages must have taken place while the family was still living at Bear Island. My mother, Sophie Potts, went to live with them. She had come from Mattawa with her brothers (Tom, Charlie and Fred Potts); since they had to work, *Koomis* (Grandmother Margaret, my dad's mother), raised her.

My father and Willie Moore, who was a long-time childhood friend, both wanted to find wives and they had heard of a pretty young girl up at Elk Lake or Matachewan. Lisa.

Their story, as my dad and mom told me: he and Willie Moore went up to look over this girl and to court her. But when they got there, Tom Seville Sr. had beat them to her. He had asked for her hand and sent her away to school until she was old enough to marry. So the disheartened young men returned to Bear Island.

When my dad got back, *Koomis* suggested he marry my mother who had been living with them. So when she was 18, they were married in Haileybury. By this time, they were living at Friday's Point. Then my dad worked hard, saved and started adding on to that log cabin my uncle had first built for *Koomis*.

My parents, Willie Friday and Sophie Potts

From what I understand, at that time the railroad and the highway to Temagami were built and the tourists were starting to holiday on the lake. Jim and Willie cut logs for Temagami Lodge. I believe they also helped build it. The first child to be born there was Jim Friday Jr. on February 28, 1917, then Jane Friday born April 14, 1920 and then me on June 11, 1931.

During World War I, Joe Friday enlisted, as did some of the other men from Bear Island. This would have been 1916. After the war, there was a terrible flu. A lot of people at Bear Island died. Joe told me he and George Turner (his nephew) would go from house to house making fires, cooking soup and doing what they could for the sick people.

After the birth of Jim and Jane, Friday's Camp was progressing. And while they were in their teens (Jim and Jane), George Friday died, leaving four boys and three girls. I was told that Uncle George was a very strong man and was taken to the New York World Fair to lift and carry 100-pound drums of flour.

1. Koomis Margaret Sanders (Friday) with her sons:
2. Willie Friday and his wife Sophie (Potts);
3. Joe Friday and his wife Eva (a nurse from England nee Vanderbilt,
they met when he was overseas in the army); 4. Jim Friday;
5. George Friday; in top right corner, a visitor

Charlotte's husband also died, leaving her with two boys and two girls. She remarried later, and so her two girls are Polsons. When this happened, Willie undertook to help raise the children, which is what was done in those days.

From what I understood, the Depression was on, but the people of Bear Island and the Fridays didn't suffer as they had plenty of moose, deer, beaver, partridge, rabbit and salted fish.

The Fridays grew potatoes, turnips and other vegetables for summer use. They also had a cow, a pig and work horses, and a donkey that Uncle Jim had traded with a Father Parage from Sandy Inlet.

In my childhood years, we were never hungry. We always had salted down fish my mom put away in the fall, and moose or deer hanging up in the trees up the hill.

Uncle Joe's deer hunt, 1918, Lake Temagami

And we had beaver that Uncle Jim and my dad caught, and rabbits that Jane and my mom snared. We also had Uncle Jim's potatoes and my dad always got a supply of flour, lard, etc. in the fall from a wholesaler in Cobalt. I still remember the spicy smells, and the smell of apples in the warehouse, where we would go, my dad, my mom and I. The man's name at the warehouse I don't know. When we went up to Cobalt, Junior Friday would come with us. My dad would give us money for lunch at the Minerva restaurant. The owners were Greek and friends of my dad. We would order hot dogs and a dish of Jell-O with whipped cream and a glass of Coke. My, that was good!

During the Depression, Willie, my dad, had professors from the universities come and stay with us and teach Jimmy, Jane and Gus, Louis and Ella Friday, and Donald Potts and Philip correspondence courses. One teacher that I remember was Ed Taggart. He received room and board and tobacco for this work.

There was another one, but I can't remember his name. He built a log cabin on the island behind Bear Island. He also collected bear skins, which Uncle Jim fixed for him. Annie Leduc told me she remembers her and her sister, Beatrice, working for my mom. She was twelve or fourteen years old and Beatrice a year older or so. Also Margaret Friday and Susie Moore, who were older.

Willie and Old Jim cut wood and filled ice houses for the camps and cottages. The boys, Jimmy, Philip, Gus, Louie and other young men would work for them. They also trapped in the winter and spring.

Willie Friday and Old Jim at camp, tending the fire

7

Jim Friday, Gus Friday and Raymond Baker

The trappers used to give me weasels that got caught in their traps. I would get 25 cents a pelt at the Hudson's Bay Company store. My mother trapped mink for her Christmas money. Jane and I would go in the canoe with her when she set out her mink traps. It helped her one year when the caretakers at Temagami Lodge tried to raise mink. A few wandered out and I guess Mom caught them.

My mother in her kitchen

At one time, my dad was also captain of the boat 'The Belle'. After church on Sunday, Mom and I would board the boat at Bear Island and go for a ride up to Sandy Inlet. This didn't happen every Sunday, only when Mom could leave the camp. I was three or four years old at the time. I also remember when I was four or five, my Aunt Charlotte coming for a visit in the summer. Also Aunt Mary, Junior and Doreen. I then had some playmates.

Bear Island Steamer 'The Belle', Lake Temagami

Part 2
Family Stories

My entry into the world

I was born in June with the help of Granny Turner, Lucy Peshabou, Flora Roy and Dr. Arnold from Haileybury, who got to Friday's Point and told the midwives I would not live. My dad's sister, Aunt Charlotte, looked after me until September while my mother recuperated. She said that her blood was low and I guess she was starting the 'change'. I was fed with an eye dropper at birth and my dad said that I had to have special formula. So when they ordered their winter staples from Cobalt, they ordered ten cases of my formula.

It was told to me, at my nephew Philip Roy's funeral by Buddy Longten (Flora Roy's daughter), that she was with her mother at Friday's Point when I was born. She said she was about 12 years old and remembers going down to the front dock to meet Dr. Arnold and to carry his bag up the hill. She remembered my birth and how small I was (3 lbs. 4 oz.) and that they wrapped me in a basket that had 'sad irons' in it in the oven door. She also remembers the doctor saying that I would not last the night. She was happy to see that I had survived and was still living.

Friday's lodge verandah, spring 1955;
back row l-r, Gus Friday, Jim Friday (Jr.), Old Peshabou, Phil Potts, Louie
Friday; front row l-r, Jim Friday, my sister Jane, my mother, me and my father

Early schooling, learning to read

My early childhood was at the Point, until I had to have schooling. Then my dad hired teachers from the Board of Education to teach me and to be hostess, secretary and bookkeeper at the camp for the summer months. He wrote to the Department of Education and the universities for this position.

They came, usually in June, and that's when I started my schooling: reading, writing, arithmetic, spelling and social studies. My days were 9 a.m. to 4:30 p.m., Monday to Friday, and sometimes Saturdays and Sundays. That was an interesting part of my life in the summer. I was schooled six days a week in the three Rs. But I could read already, as my brother and sister had taught me in the long winter months.

I was very fortunate to be able to read by the time I was four or five years old. My brother Jim and my sister Jane taught me how to read because they got tired of always having to read the weekly funny papers to me. They were teenagers, and it became a nuisance for them. I had books, comic book subscriptions sent to me from the USA by tourists who came to camp in the summer. Some had their children send me books that they didn't need anymore. We also had a newspaper called the 'Star Weekly' that had comics, like Popeye, Lil' Abner and Little Orphan Annie. I also liked Jim and Jane's school readers.

When I started my home schooling in the summer, my first teacher taught me to read, but thanks to my brother and sister, I was way ahead in my readers, so she had to order more for me!

Reading was so wonderful for me! I usually had no one my own age to play with, so it opened up a whole new world. I even used to read newspapers the tourists left in the living room.

I remember reading Old Jim's bible to him. He could read himself, but this was good reading practice for me and would get me to know the Bible stories.

One of my teachers with me at home

Another home schooling teacher, Miss Pfeiffer, and me

My dad also got me to read the Bible on Sundays. He was religious (Anglican) and took it very seriously. Sunday was a day of rest! So we had two meals on that day: a big breakfast, which he always cooked: it was pancakes, bacon or pork sausages, eggs, toast and always real maple syrup or jam, and then we'd have supper.

Even the team of horses was not allowed to work on Sunday. I remember that a jobber from Mattawa had a lumber camp in KoKoKo Bay, and his truck got stuck in the slush. He came over and asked my dad if he could drive his team to pull him out. My dad refused, even though he offered him $100. My dad explained why to Mr. Montroy and told him that there was a team at Bear Island. Mr. Montroy praised him for his convictions and they parted friends.

More family stories

I mentioned that my dad cut wood and filled ice houses for camps on the lake. I remember I used to take a hot meal in a lunch box tied to a sled, with one dog, usually *Mukoons*, pulling me and the lunch over to where they were working on Temagami Island (behind the light). I would have lunch with them and then hitch a ride home or take the dog sled and go and visit Joe Gouroux and his wife (at Katchinanys Island, now). I was never afraid, as I had my big black dog with me.

My sister Jane and I also used to help Uncle Jim with the winter net. In the fall, he would put two long poles in the water, where he planned to set the net. There was a long line on these poles. When the lake froze over and when it was strong enough to walk on, Jane and I would go down to Spawning Bay with Uncle Jim to set the net, which my mom got ready, with a stick on the top and stones on the bottom. When we got to where the poles were, he would cut holes along where the line with the net goes through.

A long pole was used to pull the net that was tied to the line and pull it taut out on the ice where the poles were. The one on shore was secured. Then when we came back a few days later, we would take the line down from the pole out in the ice and walk and pull it while Uncle Jim took the fish out of the net. When the net was all out, it went back down the hole, only now the line pulled it and we didn't need the pole.

Spawning Narrows would be open in late March or April, and on Sundays, my mom would pack a lunch and we would all walk down there, and her and my dad would pick up the net they had set across the narrows. Then we would have fresh fried fish and my dad would make a bannock. If Pa was not there, then Uncle Charley would make one. The net would dry and then was reset again. Old Jim was always afraid of the game wardens, but most of the time he was spring trapping with my dad. The lake was also getting bad, but we had a bush trail. It was so nice to see that bit of open water, we knew that summer was not far off.

Jumping ahead in time… Don, my late husband, watched a family of otters playing at that same spot. They would slide down the icy rock into the little spot of open water. Don and I had taken the canoe down in preparation to set a net. My mom's grandchildren all got to enjoy this adventure and Verna and Baptese named it 'Grandma's Narrows'. To this day, we still call it that when we talk amongst ourselves of the good times we had there.

Another adventure that I remember when I was a child was one Easter, when my mom, my dad and I went down to the point past the pump house (towards Ketchinanys Island). The lake was candle ice, so my dad felt safe from the game warden to do what we were going to do. He got a big fire going and Mom singed a moose nose and we cleaned it. Then Mom put it in a big pot. She used the number ten lard pail and boiled it all afternoon. The moose tongue was soaking in salt water. Then it was cooked and we had moose tongue and *moosediscut*, the long gut of the moose cleaned and smoked. We also had boiled moose ribs. What a feast! June and Margaret McCauley came over. I remember Margaret McCauley was all dressed up in a shiny dress and red shoes. Then Uncle came and Charley. We ate and ate, it all tasted so good. By this time, it was getting dark, but everyone was full and back to the house we all went.

This was in the spring, when the snow was gone and the ice on the lake was black ice. Mom was spring cleaning, so she had Margaret Quinn working for her. Margaret was later married to Raymond Becker. She was also related to Mom's cousin Flora McCauly. She and Margaret Quinn were sisters. Flora and her kids, Billy, George and Doreen used to visit us in the summer. I just remember it was fun when these relatives came to visit Aunty Mary from Temagami with Junior and Doreen. Then Auntie Charlotte, Pa's sister, Uncle Joe's twin, would come. Plus all the tourists. It was a busy time!

Mom told me that when *Koomis*, my dad's mother died, he and his brothers were heartbroken. She died in February, in what Mom called the little living room. I have her bed in Callander and as a child I slept on it. She, *Koomis*, is buried on Bear Island beside her husband, John Friday. After her death, my dad and his brothers Joe and Jim and my mom, along with Jim and Jane (my brother and sister, who were kids then) took off on the Quebec side. La Sarre is where they went. On the way, Aunty Charlotte, Alex and their kids joined them. They were gone all summer. I guess that was a way of handling their grief.

Margaret Friday, Jane Roy and Doreen Friday, with the cabins in the background

When I was old enough, about seven or eight years old, my mother and sister would make big birthday parties for me. They did all the inviting and if the 11th of June fell on a school day, Dad would speak to the priest and the kids would get the day off. He would go over in the 'big boat' and pick them all up. The one time that I remember, Junior Friday and Ella were at the camp. Junior and I got dressed in our best clothes and went down to meet my guests.

We played all kinds of games and there were prizes. We played the old player piano and then opened my gifts. I remember that I got a Shirley Temple doll and another year I got a record player and records. One record that I remember was 'A Froggy Went a Courting'. I don't remember what we ate, but I do remember that we had a huge layered birthday cake and inside, wrapped in wax paper, were fortunes, charms and money. I remember that Agnes Katt swallowed a dime. And I remember Barbara Turner, her sisters, Tilley Potts, Chuck Turner, Davey Missabi and his sisters and others coming to my party.

Ricky Best (son of Dr. Best who invented insulin) and me,
with Uncle's potato garden in the background

I also remember that the year I got the Shirley Temple doll, I left it on the veranda and *Mukoons* chewed it up! That was a disaster. Tilley still remembers my parties.

Little People

When I was about four years old, maybe five, my mother told me about the Little People. I was very small as a child and I had no playmates my age, only my brother and sister who were teenagers. My imagination was my companion. Mom told me to be very careful when I was by myself in the woods, as there were Little People (*ga gashing Anishnaabe*) who would be tempted to take me away with them. They may have played with me, as I had a pretend playmate. One of the men who worked for my father said he heard me conversing with someone in the bush. I was very angry when he told my mother this.

My cousin Junior spent that summer with us. We often went, him and I, to the woods, and my mom would tell us if they came to play with us not to go with them, as they liked to play with children.

I have heard so many stories about these little *Anishnaabe*, and how only children see them. I've asked Elders about them, and they do exist. At some feasts, the Elder puts a plate out for them where they are known to live. One place I heard of was Serpent River in north-western Ontario. When highway 17 was being built, the Elders, seniors and residents asked the Department of Highways to change the route, as they were going to blast where these Little People lived. They had a meeting and the route was changed. I think about this when I pass Serpent River.

At Bear Island, I have heard stories about a young girl who was going with her family in their boat. She forgot something in the house, so she ran back up the hill. On the way up, she ran into a Little Person who was dressed in bush clothes and had a bow and arrows. No words were spoken.

I also have a friend who says her sister has a pair living at her house. This friend stayed overnight with me and said I have Little People here, as she heard them running around in my living room and it woke her up. When she went home, I was tidying up and looked in my candy dish (which had a cover on it). I found wrappers and there were only about a dozen Hershey's Kisses left in the dish. The next time I was taking on the phone with this friend, I asked her if she enjoyed the candy.

She said she never liked chocolate. So I guess they had a good treat. The next time her and her nephew came and stayed overnight, her nephew couldn't find his bracelet that he put on the coffee table. We searched, but it never turned up! Little People like shiny things and candy.

Another friend told me about her dad's team of horses. He went to the barn in the morning and the team of horses had their manes and tails all colourfully braided with yarn. That night, he undid the braids, and the next morning, they were all colourfully braided again. I have heard many more similar stories, but these came to mind.

Trapping at the 'Little Camp'

When I was six, maybe seven years old, my dad took me with him and Uncle Jim trapping at the 'Little Camp'. Only there was no cabin then at Crash Lake. We used a cabin on Chambers Lake. I skated down to Spawning portage and then Uncle Jim, my dad and I and a dog team were on our way.

The first night out we met Jimmy and Louie Friday at Crash Lake. (In later years, he built a trap cabin there.) We camped in the hollow of a huge pine tree that had fallen near the lake. We were up all night 'trenching' beaver. Jimmy and Louie came during that night, and then they *azhkaed*. That is to say, they went around the pond where there was a beaver house or two and sounded out where the beaver had an entrance to his lodge. They used a dog that was good at sniffing beaver for this.

This was Jimmy's dog *Mukoons* (also spelled *makoons*, which means "little bear"): he would smell out the beavers and then they'd set traps at the entrance to the tunnels. So they took the dog and patrolled the area. I went with Jimmy and *Mukoons* put his head down one of the holes. Jimmy gave me a fish fork and I felt the beaver's tail. He then reached in and pulled the beaver out and killed it.

It was not a very big pond where this was done. When we caught one, Louie and I walked back to camp where we skinned it, cut it up and put it on to boil. He also made a bannock, leaning the cast iron pan up by the fire to cook it. While we had our backs turned, *Mukoons* ate it! Hot as it was. So Louie made another one, and this time I kept watch while it cooked. The beaver was cooking and so were its tail, heart and liver. They were the first to be ready.

By this time, my dad, Jimmy and Uncle Jim all came back, ready to eat and then to go catch more beaver. This method was illegal and it was not on all lakes that were you able to do this. This was way after midnight. I went to bed in the sleeping bag my dad had fixed up for me on some spruce boughs. Pa laid down the spruce boughs and a tarp and then our sleeping bags. The fire, a big one, was at our feet. I didn't undress, just took off my moccasins and jacket. This was my first time sleeping outdoors in the winter.

I remember that I slept well and the next morning, Uncle Jim and I broke camp and walked to an old prospector's cabin at Chambers Lake, while my dad went to set out more traps. We made a big fire and swept out the cabin and found that I had lost my shoes. So we back tracked. Uncle didn't say much to me but we found them all!

Pa joined us later and Louie and Jimmy went on to his trapping ground at *Macobe*. Pa would trap and Uncle and I would get wood, set rabbit snares and set the fishing net. (He had put the poles for the net in the lake in the fall.) Then when Pa got back at night, he cooked supper. Uncle made more of a mess when he did the cooking. It's an experience I had, and I will always remember it.

We stayed out for about ten or twelve days. Till I got too lonesome for my mom and Jane. The trapping clothes my dad had bought for me for this trip, my boy's britches, boy's laced rubber boots and leather jacket we later gave to Ronnie Turner.

In later years, my dad built a log cabin at Crash Lake (a plane went down on this lake). Don and I went up and finished it after we were married. I guess that was my honeymoon. The year was 1948.

The log cabin built by my dad and others; I am there with one of my teachers, and with "Pop" Muir from Buffalo (standing) who would come over to Friday's camp and make ice cream and play the tuba

Later on, Don, myself, Rick, Rob and Don (junior) went up to the cabin in the winter time and also in the fall. We had good times up there. Don also used to take Dupont co-workers fishing for bass there. After my dad died, the trapping grounds were passed on to Uncle Charlie (Mom's brother). Then after he died, it was passed on to Gus Friday. Then he died, and Tom Friday now traps it.

Watching beavers

Three of four miles from Friday's Camp, there was a lake called Williams Lake. It was really a large pond that the beavers had dammed up. Also, growing there were cranberries, which my family always picked in the fall. My dad would go there in the morning and take down some of the beaver dam. That evening, he would take some of the guests who were interested in the 'Launch' (a big engine-powered boat) to go and see the beaver at work rebuilding the dam.

This was always a big hit with the guests, especially if there was an engineer among them. It would be at least a two-hour show. The beavers acted as if they were stars. My das also showed the guests where the cranberries grew. Some of the people had never seen where cranberries grow. The beavers amazed the people with how quickly they put the dam back together. I would often go with my dad and the guests. Even I was amazed at the beavers' building abilities.

Going to school in North Bay

In 1940, when I was nine years old, I came to North Bay to go to school. I lived with a Mrs. Kirk on Regina Street. Pa had written to the rector of St. John's Anglican Church for someone to room and board me. They also had to be Anglican. She was a very nice lady. I went to Dr. Caruthers School, also known as Brook Street School.

When I was sent to North Bay to school, I had our school library. One of the teachers took me to the public library to show me how to use my membership card and take out books. I felt like I was in heaven! I loved reading history and geography. Science, I was not too interested in. I think that my love for reading helped me adjust to living away from home. I was always going to the library for books. They were my 'company' and friends. I did make friends after about a month.

I had pretty good grades in history, geography and literature in my school days. Even in those days, I loved to write stories. Anything to do with my history and geography notes. And as I grew up, I continued to enjoy reading. I still love to read. I hope my great-grandchildren will like to read as much as I did. I gave them books as gifts instead of toys.

My first teacher was a Miss Forest in grade four. I felt so alone. I didn't know anyone but I could do the reading, arithmetic, writing and spelling. For the history and geography, I had to catch up. Recess would find me outside, sitting on the front door steps, crying silently to myself. A girl in my class called Gloria came and comforted me and helped me. I stayed at Mrs. Kirk's for about a month or so.

Then I moved to Mosley Williams' on McIntyre and went to McIntyre School. Also, there was a girl, a year older, whose name was Elizabeth. The mother and father were English people, and they were very strict with us! No talking at meal time. If you got giggly, you were sent to the kitchen to eat alone. There was a teenager, Gerald, who got Elizabeth and me in trouble at meal time. So she and I ate alone in the kitchen a lot. From there, I stayed with the MacKenny's and Standish.

After that, I stayed with a Mrs. Tilley, and then at my best friend Ruth Thompson's home. I liked it there as I was like one of the family. I went to church at St. John's at 9 a.m., then taught Sunday school and at night sang in the choir. I was a Brownie till I was ten years old, then went into the Girl Guides. I was also in our school choir.

On Saturdays after our chores, we were allowed to go out to the show. Sometimes we went skating or sliding. In spring, we went to ball games, we went swimming or we played scrub with other kids. We also went to a lot of concerts at the Capitol Theatre. I remember going to see Oscar Peterson and the Von Trapp family, the family that was in The Sound of Music. We saw them shopping in Eaton's store. They were dressed in their country's national costume.

Sometimes, we played hooky from school, but it was no fun because if we went on Main Street, too many people knew the Thompsons. We never did get found out though.

On V-day (Second World War), we were allowed to stay out and watch people dancing in the street, drinking. Everybody was so happy! We also went to St. John's church. If we didn't, Mrs. T would have had a fit.

During my first year at school in North Bay, I was always looking forward to the holidays. The first year I went home for Christmas, I travelled on the O.N.R. train that left North Bay at 8 a.m. and arrived in Temagami at 10 a.m. I was met at the station by John Turner, my Dad's nephew, whom I was to travel with. I was also travelling with his son, his daughter who was in the Air Force and my brother's sister-in-law who was also in the Air Force. We went to Finlayson Park where we all got into a boat. This was December 21st or 22nd and the lake was still open! We all huddled under tarps to keep warm and dry. The water splashed on the tarps and froze. We were kept dry and warm though. I was the first to disembark. So glad to be home! The lake froze a few days later. This was one time my dad didn't get to go to Haileybury for Christmas church services.

Another Christmas holiday, the cars were travelling over the frozen lake. I got off the train with my cousin, so we hired a taxi to take us up the lake. We got as far as what is known as Skull Narrows. The road was snowed in as it had started to storm! We got out and started to walk. We were both dressed for the weather. We left our luggage as the taxi would deliver it when it was possible. We just wanted to get home. We were warmly dressed and it was before noon. It was stormy, cold and windy. We parted, my cousin going to Bear Island, following the road where he could see it. I found a car track and followed it to my home at Friday's Point. Imagine my parents' surprise when a snowman walked in! They said "Why didn't you stay over in Temagami and wait till the next day?" I wanted to be home.

Then the first year I came home for Easter, I was unable to get back to school on time in North Bay. My dad and brother were out trapping for the spring hunt. The ice had gone from along the shore. My mother decided we would paddle over to Bear Island to see her friend Margaret, who was my dad's nephew's wife. We made it over, and Mom and Margaret decided they would paddle to Temagami so that I could get back to school, as I had missed ten days already. So we all went back to the camp.

Margaret, her daughter Nellie, Mom and I started out the next morning at 9 a.m., Mom in the stern, Margaret in the bow. They changed places later in the day.

It was nice and sunny with a slight breeze. We stopped and had lunch at Tetapaga Creek. The moms talked over what route we would take, as the ice was moving and closing up the open waters where we were on the north shore. They could see the south shore was open. So they decided we would cross over.

I was put in the front, and when they ran the canoe onto the ice, I was to get out (I was the lightest) and pull the canoe, and they would use their paddles to push. The ice was what was called 'candle ice' (a form of rotten ice that water can seep through), it was still strong enough for me to walk on and pull the canoe with their help. We made it to the open water, and continued on our way over the open water.

The ice was now moving and piling up on the north shore. We were just getting in the narrows and didn't have far to go. The five o'clock whistle blew at the mill. For me, that was quite an experience. It showed me what determination those two women had. Women can do anything that they make up their mind to do.

My mother at Friday's Point

Another holiday adventure happened at Easter, many years later. That time, I got off the train and went over to my cousin's who told me that my dad said that I was to go see his nephew John Turner and go up the lake with him. I was to travel lightly, leave my suitcase with my cousin, and dress warm. I went and located my dad's nephew and he told me to meet him down at the boat dock and bring a lunch and no luggage. I went to the restaurant and got a sandwich and an apple.

We left at about 10:30 a.m. and it was a cloudy day. The ice was 'candle ice'. Mr. Turner asked me if I could walk, as he could carry me or pull me in the little sled he had. We started out, and he told me to stay behind the sled he was pulling. We got about half way up and stopped for our lunch. He said I was doing pretty good, keeping up with him. He now asked me what I would do if the ice gave way and he went in.

He was a big man, at least six feet tall and about 275 pounds. I said I would push the sled toward him and that he would be able to crawl out. He asked me if I would get scared and run away, and I said "No," because I had to do what I could to get him out. We started out again and he said for me to stay back further from the sled. It was now late afternoon, and still a dark day.

When we were walking, the water was seeping up (this is candle ice). We walked faster. We were now getting to the narrows called Skull Narrows. As we were nearing the narrows, there was my dad, standing on the shore, yelling for us to get off the ice. He had cut a tree down so that we could walk on it to get to shore. I went first as I was the lightest. I was so glad to see my dad! He had phoned Millers Drugstore and they told him they heard I was walking up the lake with Turner's son. That was frightening news for him, as I had done that before. He was glad to see it was John Turner himself! So we walked the bush trail. Mr. Turner continued on to Bear Island and got off the ice at a camp called Denten's. That year, I didn't get back to school on time. I was two weeks late due to the breakup of the ice on the lake. What times I had to get home!

When I was older, I went to North Bay Collegiate and Vocational School for a few months. Then I quit and went home because Don and I wanted to get married. I knew my dad would say I was too young. I took a correspondence course and the HBC's wife helped me with the course. I had to have eight lessons of each subject in the mail for one week: math, history, geography and English.

When an Indian baby is born

When an Indian baby is born, an animal comes to visit or to greet the newborn. This is called *Wiisanna*. My Uncle Joe and Aunty Charlotte were twins, and when they were born, twin caribou visited outside their shelter.

When I was born, my mom said a partridge came to visit. My first born son had a fox visit, and Uncle Jim said it was a bad omen. He tried to kill the fox but couldn't. My brother's first born, Billy, had a squirrel. It was February and was considered bad luck too. You had to be aware of these visits and take notice.

When Louise was born she had a turtle. Her mother would put her in her bassinette in a playpen outside. This was in June or July and Martha would find a turtle in the playpen. It really frightened her. Jimmy and Mickey put an X in white paint on it and took it in the boat to the Southwest Arm. She put Louise out the next day, thinking the turtle was 20 miles away, but when she looked out to check on her, there was the turtle. So she just let it visit. The turtle is good luck and a long life.

For my boys, Rob, Don and Rick, I know that one was a muskrat, in the ditch at Mill Road. Rick was loons up at Grandma's. For Don and Melissa, I can't remember or I was not aware of those things at that time.

When spring came

After the lumber camp in Spawning Bay, in the spring, there was what they called a 'bush camp' about five or six miles northeast from the Point. Young men cleaned up the brush where they had cut trees.

Everyone, my dad, Jim, Philip and Louie were spring hunting and Mom, Jane, Marg Potts, Johnny Paul and Old Jim were at the camp. We were tired of eating fish, so Mom sent Uncle up to the bush camp with a sack of cleaned fish to trade for some fresh meat and tobacco for Uncle. The ice was bad, so we couldn't go to Bear Island. He came back with pork chops and sausage. Boy did that taste good. Not long after, my dad came home with fresh beaver. The lake was open by then. Mom, Jane and Margaret had the rooms ready for the spring fishermen.

I remember the Brown girls form Keewatin Camp spent the break-up with us because the ice was too weak up the north arm. I think one of them was Helen and the other, I can't remember her name. Mom had them help with spring cleaning, and getting the cabins ready, and rooms for the spring fishermen. Jane and Jimmy were teenagers, as were the Brown girls. So they had a lot of fun! It was a busy time at the camp, getting boats and motors ready for summer and watching the ice pile up on the shore or docks – when it started moving.

There were a lot of people at the camp: Louie, Margaret, Uncle Charley, sometimes Jamesey Petrant and Uncle Alex from Notre-Dame-du-Nord. Mom and the women washed blankets, cleaned and painted, waxed floors and cleaned all the windows.

For me, it was exciting to have all these people around, even though I had no one to play with. I guess I was a nuisance at times. So one of those time, I went and got a dip net and caught butterflies and put them in a cabin room. I had caught hundreds of those yellow and black ones and orange and black ones. I got tired of catching them, but I didn't tell Mom where I put them. The next day, she went to check the rooms in the cabin. What a surprise when she opened the door! I don't think I got heck, but it was a good laugh. I do remember having to help her chase them out!

In the spring, when my dad would be away spring trapping with Jimmy, Philip and Old Jim, we would be left alone at the camp with mom's brother, Uncle Charley. On a Sunday afternoon, Mom would pack a lunch box and we would all walk down to Spawning Narrows, or as Verna, Tommy and Baptese would call it: 'Grandma's Bay'.

The narrows would be open and this is where a net was set and a canoe was kept. We would pick the net up and Uncle Charlie and Mom or Dad would clean the fish. Then we had fresh fried fish, bannock and warmed potatoes for our lunch. The net was washed and dried to be set again. This was our first canoe ride. It was a relaxing afternoon. There was one time that I remember - I must have been four or five years old - my dad was there and Jane pushed me in the water. It was an accident. I guess I must have been teasing her. Anyway, a fire was made and they dried my clothes. I was wrapped in Pa's coat. But I still had a good time. This outing we kept up for years. Verna, Tom, Baptese and Louise still remember these outings.

During the spring, before the ice went off the lake, this is when my mom and dad had extra people work for them to get ready for the spring fishermen and summer tourists. There were rooms to houseclean and new paint to put on. With Pa, it was boats to be varnished. Uncle Jim and Charley would mend and paint the canvas and skiffs. Jimmy, Louie and Phillip would be away for the spring hunt, which was for beaver and muskrat.

I remember when my mom, Jane and Margaret Trepanier, would paint the living room floor. I should say varnish. It had to dry for at least two days. So at night, we would climb up a ladder on the side of the house to go upstairs to our bedrooms. That, I thought, was so much fun.

I also remember one spring time when Jimmy's pet bear *M'kwa* awoke from his sleep in the ice house. First he chased Jane and Lena Petrant and they were in the outhouse until someone heard them yelling. Then the bear was swinging in Ma's fish net and tore it. Then after they got him untangled, the bear climbed the ladder to the roof.

That was it for the bear. They had to shoot him because he was too mischievous!

M'kwa going up the ladder to the roof

My dad and me with the bear skin

Summer time

In the summer of 1935 or 1936, my cousin Junior, who was nine or ten, spent the summer with me. Our time was spent swimming, playing with boats that we made ourselves out of used worm boxes that we used as cabins and boathouses. We also caught minnows and we made our own hooks. We used head pins that we bent and put small pieces of worm on them. The line was the finest fish line. We saved the minnows we caught and sold them to the tourists for 25 cents a dozen. We also dug up and gathered worms that we sold. On rainy nights, we went out with a flashlight and caught big fat night crawlers.

One day I was running with my fishing rod, a willow pole with a real hook to catch bass, and I caught my own leg. Up to the house we ran. My cousins and sister looked at my hooked leg, told my mother to get iodine, a file and pliers. They put me on the table in the living room and poured iodine on my leg. I fainted and while I was unconscious, she took the hook out.

I came to on the front veranda, a bandage on my leg and ready to go again. I limped around for a few days, but I healed quickly. I still have a tiny scar.

My cousin who doctored me was quite the lady. She helped bring babies into the world, but also nursed people who were at the end of their lives. She also helped prepare the dead for funerals. When we went to the lake, playing or swimming, we also went into the woods and played camping. We also spent time picking blueberries. We were never afraid of bears.

One time, we found a nest of baby partridge. Each took one to show Uncle. Well, we were given a long lecture on not taking baby wildlife because the mother would disown the babies because we handled them and our scent was on them.

But we could take them back, and before we put them in their nests, we must take cedar, rub it on our hands and brush the babies with the cedar. This might take away our human scents and the mother would accept them. Never again did we make that big mistake! We even gave up chasing baby ducks and putting them on a paddle.

We never picked them out of the water, but the mother duck would chase us in our canoe.

That's me, in a canoe

One evening, after supper, we took our row boat and went fishing at Grandma's Narrows. Our fishing rod was a willow pole and we had our minnows. We were having so much fun catching fish. We never counted them.

We had an old tub we were putting them in, so our boat wouldn't get slimy and fishy! It was starting to be dusk and along came Louie Friday in a canoe, asking what did we think we were doing, not telling anyone where we were going, and what were we doing with all that fish? So we pulled up our anchor, rolled in our fishing lines and back home we rowed. We knew we were in trouble!

We got home and my parents and Uncle gave us a good talking to about all the fish we caught and not asking if we could go fishing! My cousin Louie cleaned the fish with our help. We were told the next day we were to put our fish on ice, row to all the camps near us and give away our fish, without taking money or treats, and not come back until all the fish was gone. My Dad would check up on us by going to where and who we gave our fish to. Believe me, we never did that again. Our row boat lay idle for a while after all the rowing we did!

Louie Friday, my cousin, was so tall that he had to bend his head to go through some doorways at the camp. He was also very strong. When I was small (five or six years old) I'd grab onto one of his arms and he would lift me high up. He had only one eye. He lost his eye opening a sack of potatoes when he was just a young man. He loved to tease and joke. And he was a good cook. He never married, but he loved kids. The tourists always wanted him as their guide year after year. When they had the Regatta at Cochrane Camp, he usually won the single guide race. I have a '1st' medal that he gave me. He was killed by a hit and run driver in May. He never got to see my Doug, as he had gone trapping when my son was born.

Louie Friday and Johnny Marks with a big catch

Preparing for ice fishing in the fall

Each fall, Uncle Jim would go down to Loon Bay to set the poles in where he would set the fish net once the lake froze. My mom got the net ready, with a stick on the top and stones on the bottom. A line was attached by one person to the poles as the net would be tied on at one end. A second person would pull the end of the line that was not attached, and under the ice it would go. When the lake froze over, my sister and I were always the ones to accompany Uncle Jim.

Walking on the newly frozen ice was always an experience. We trusted our uncle to sound the ice for safe walking. Once we got to where the poles were set in the frozen lake, Uncle would chop a hole where the pole was at the shore. My sister and I would then chop one at the second pole. Uncle would then yell at us to start pulling the line. He had tied the net on the line and we were to pull it slowly while he put the net in the water. I would walk back to shore where he was. My sister would stay by the hole, and when she'd see the line with the net, she would grab it and Uncle would go and secure it to the pole like he did with the net at the shore. The string I had been pulling was then attached to the pole or a bush on the shore.

When this was done, back home we would go, until a day or so later, when we'd go back to see how many fish we caught. Uncle would pull the net in at the shore. The line I had attached to a bush or to the pole would be stretched out on the snow and as Uncle pulled the net it would go back in the hole where my sister watched it. One he got to the end of the net, he would untangle it and start re-setting it, with my sister pulling the line to get the net back in the water.

I would help with the line because it would freeze and get iced up. My job was to take as much of the ice off as I could. Then home we would go with our fish, looking forward to fresh fish for supper. My sister and I always enjoyed this chore. To us, it wasn't a chore, it was an exciting trip, wondering how many fish we had caught. This job was always done by us three: Uncle, sister and me!

Winter stories

Years ago, in 1935 or 1936, there was a winter road that ran by the point to Spawning Lake, where the lumber camp was. They had a bush road to Temagami. It came out between Goward and Temagami. This road was well marked and the lumber camp was always good for a stop for "tea" and lunch, and lots of it! I can remember the "cookie" giving me big cookies and milk. It was called Klim powdered milk, but boy was it good!

The road to Temagami was 'iced'. The horses hauled their big load of logs to Gowards. There were no logging trucks in those days, only horses. When there was an accident with the horses, they would sell them or give them away for dog food. I remember coming with my dad and my sister Jane and Raymond Becker with one or two dog teams. When we got to the place we called Grandma's Narrows, the short portage was dark. Raymond lit some birch trees and we could see our way. We always walked behind the dogs in the bush. On the lake you could ride if the trail was good. The mailman would use this road, as would the men who hauled freight for the HBC. So the road to Bear Island was really good for us at Friday's.

Many, many years later, cars would travel on the ice from Temagami. When the ice was strong enough, traffic on the lake was busy. The lumber camps were in different locations now that vehicles were used. Jane cooked one year at a camp in Kokoko Bay for Turcottes from Mattawa.

We spent one winter at Bear Island in the Hudson Bay House, down from George Turner's. I always wondered why we spent the winter there. I was only about four or five years old. Jane and Jimmy were teenagers, along with Gus, Ella and Phillip who needed help with their correspondence courses. There was a man and his wife teaching at Bear Island. Their names were Mr. and Mrs. MacKash.

I would go to Sunday school along with the other kids. That Christmas we had a party and George Turner was Santa. Barbara Turner got so frightened she ran out screaming with her mom behind her! What excitement. I always played with her and was always told not to stay at her house for supper because they had a lot of kids to feed. But I always managed to get asked to stay. We would have boiled beans with corn syrup in them, with bannock. I thought this was great! When I got called home it wasn't so great!

Barbara and I were also told not to go and visit Mrs. Joe Lanois. She lived up the hill from George's house. We used to sneak up there and knock on her door. She would give us a big homemade cookie to get rid of us until the next time. But our mothers heard about it and put an end to it.

My mother at Friday's Point in winter

When we lived at Bear Island, they had a dance at the HBC. George Linklater was the store manager. Tarps were hung around, covering the store shelves. The counters were shoved into the corner for the coats. This is where the small kids were put to sleep out of the way of the dancers.

Barbara and I used to go and play with Linklater's sons, Tommy and Eddy. Eddy drowned years later at 'Rabbit Nose'. I was also taken to a wake in a cabin behind Tom Potts' house. It was for a Paul girl, I think her name was Lily. Barb would come to our house and we were given old dresses and other clothes, and we could dress up in them. I had lots of toys as tourists sent me Christmas gifts.

Christmas, I remember...

a
Merry Christmas
and a
Happy New Year

Mrs. Sophie Friday

Friday' Camps, Temagami, Ontario

Friday's Christmas postcard; on the right, Larry Turner's dog sled

When I was four years old or so (I think I was), my mother, Pa, Jane and me used to go to Haileybury for Christmas. My dad was a very devout Anglican, and him and Ma liked going to midnight mass at either Haileybury or Cobalt. We would go by horse sleigh or dog sled the day before Christmas Eve. Old Jim stayed home and he would go to Old Charlie Moore's or to John Turner's. Or stay home. Uncle and Jimmy stayed home.

Weeks before, Ma and my sister Jane baked Christmas cakes, usually a light one and a dark one. And before we left, they would also bake cookies. They would put the cakes in five-pound lard pails and try to hide them on Jimmy, Gus, Louie and Phillip, who would ask me if I knew where they were 'hid'. Jimmy, especially, was always trying to find Jane's hiding spot. He usually tried to bribe me to see if I knew her hiding place. Most times, I never knew.

Ma and Jane would also clean the front room and wash the curtains. Jane always got the tree – her and my dad. She never liked the one Jimmy or Pa brought home, it wouldn't pass her inspection. So I would go with her and Pa. My mother would have the front room all polished and the lace curtains hung up.

The front room

I would also leave cookies for Santa. In later years, I found out Uncle Jim ate them and put tracks on the roof and in the fireplace (Santa's tracks).

The big stove in the front room would be heating up the room and everything smelled clean and the balsam tree smelled nice and looked

41

as good as the decorated trees you see nowadays with lights, even if we didn't have any. Just glass ornaments, glass beads, icicles and silver garlands. There were red and green bells and streamers put up as well. Very festive! Jane did this as long as I can remember. We also got lots of mail. Even I would have parcels and cards form the tourists.

Then on the 22nd or 23rd, away we would go by dog sled, horse team or car. We would stay at the Haileybury Hotel. When in Haileybury, we would visit Senator Gordon McConkey. Lots of treats there! Mr. McConkey and Mr. Day, who used to come up deer hunting, were owners (or something like that) of the hotel. I always got real neat gifts from them.

My dad would have Aunty Charlotte and Beatrice, Annie and Gloria over for Christmas dinner at the hotel. Mom would put on my new beaded slippers that Aunt Mary or Granny Turner had made for me. I always got new slippers (moccasins) for years, until I went away to North Bay. Santa didn't even come until we got back to Friday's after Boxing Day. I only got a stocking at the hotel. And when we got back to Friday's, Santa would have come! So I was always anxious to be the first one in the house to see what Santa left under the tree. Uncle Jim was glad when we got back with lots of goodies and presents.

If Auntie Charlotte and the others didn't come to the hotel, we would go and see her in North Temiskaming. I used to like going to see her. It was more fun! Aunty was always so glad to see us, and she would cook a big meal for my dad and us.

I remember my Uncle Charley bringing the mail before Christmas and most of the parcels would be for me! The post office was jammed one year with parcels for me from the tourists who sent me dolls, toys, books, etc. My mom had put most of it away. Just too, too much. One time, I got a big 24-inch black doll, and Jane was teasing me that it looked like me. I got mad and found the hammer and busted it up. Then I got in trouble for doing that!

We would have a big meal the next day, after we got back from our Christmas visits. Sometimes, it would be a turkey but most times it would be roast beaver with stuffing. Then the turkey would be for New Years, when we would have lots of people visiting and staying for supper.

After a winter storm, snow up to the roof at Friday's Point!

There was also the Christmas that the cars were running over the ice. Omer Perrin brought me a huge parcel he delivered from Haileybury from Mr. McConkey and Mr. Day. It was a new snowsuit. When I opened the box, a toy frog jumped out. I also got a huge doll with hair and moving eyes.

We also used to visit Wes Gordon in Haileybury. He was the MP for Timiskaming. His daughters would make a big fuss over my moccasins and find treats for me. If the cars were running on the ice, we had a lot of visitors on Saturdays and Sundays.

When I was about 10 years old (I was at school in North Bay), I was coming home for Christmas. I was to go to where Kay and Philip were living in Temagami, as he was going to bring me up the lake by dog team. I was also to go and get Baptese who was at his Grandma Roy's. Baptese was about 18 months old then. So over I went and got him, and took him back to Kay's. I dug through my clothes, as he didn't have enough warm clothes. I got him ready in my sweaters, stockings and socks. He had a snowsuit, but I knew he needed more warm stuff. Philip wrapped him in a blanket and tarp in the toboggan to keep him warm. It took about two or three hours to travel up the lake.

Jane Roy with her son Baptese, older in this picture, 1948

When we got to the camp, Baptese made strange with Mom and Pa, and Uncle Jim scared him at first, but by the end of the week he was secure with us. The next day, Mom sent me to the store to buy clothes for him and Santa Claus toys. I put a blue toque on him and showed him what he looked like in the mirror. At first he didn't like it, but when he saw Pa wearing one to bed, he had to wear his to bed too. Baptese called Pa 'Bah-Bah' and the hound dogs 'gool a gools'. Old Jim was 'Unca'. He made our Christmas. We didn't get too many toys that year, but we enjoyed the tree, the clothes and the few toys we had.

At Bear Island, people would celebrate what they called 'Little Christmas', the first Sunday after New Year's. Everybody brought baked beans, bread, bannock and Christmas cake. It was a big supper, and then after they would clear the hall (at John Turner's) and dance all night. Afterwards, the families would leave Bear Island to go to their trapping grounds 'till spring, and some would stay 'till the lake opened up.

Rabbit hunting

In the winter, part of our diet was rabbit stew. So at an early age, I was taught how to set a snare. When I caught my first rabbit, I was also taught how to skin it. I watched my mom cut it and how she cooked it in an iron pot. She dredged it with white flour, salt and pepper and browned it in bacon grease.

Me and my mom with a rabbit skin blanket in front of the cabins, 1935

Then in went the rabbit with onion pieces and salt pork. It was covered with water, and cooked slowly on the stove top or put in the oven for two and a half to three hours, depending on size. When it was well done, Mom made dumplings on top of the cooked rabbit. We also ate the head, the heart and the kidneys. The skin was turned inside out, scraped and hung out in the cold. Some people tanned them and made a rabbit blanket, which was nice and warm. We also used our rabbit hides for lining our moccasins and mitts.

My uncle and I saved the rabbit ears and when we had enough, we toasted them over red coals in the wood stove. The hair burned off and they curled up when cooked. We salted them and it was just like the pork rinds that you buy today. That was our treat. My cousin and I set out snares and it was a contest to see who snared the most. My uncle from Bear Island would come down our way, but we had our area. The trick was to get up as early as we could to go see our snares. Sometimes, Mr. Fox would get there before us, but not too often.

My dad and I used to set rabbit snares across from the camp and in down to Cook's Island. He once showed me how to set snares using 'Hudson Bay' line and a spring pole.

The Hudson Bay Company had string that had many uses for trappers and everyone. One time, my dad used a willow (switch) that was near the rabbit path. He made a snare out of the string, bent the willow down, and anchored it.

The next day, I was so anxious to see if it worked. I went ahead in my snowshoes and there was a rabbit in the snare, but he was alive and hopping around. Dad took off his snowshoes to whack at the rabbit, but the rabbit would jump out of his way. The springy willow worked well as the rabbit bounced way up high, out of my dad's reach to whack him with the snowshoe. I was lying in the snow, laughing my head off.

But then he told me "Hold down the willow," and a whack with the snowshoe ended Mr. Rabbit's life. On the way home, Dad said to me "Don't tell Mama what happened." I kept my promise, but I didn't like that and I never tried to set that kind of snare again. This story is actually hilarious when told in Ojibwe.

Storytelling *(caadsooked)*

When I was four years old, I loved hearing stories my parents would tell me. The ones I enjoyed the most were the ones Uncle Jim would tell. After supper, I would ask him if I could come over to his cabin. He had a separate cabin where he slept, and where he made axe handles and other tools. He always told me stories in the Ojibwe language. These stories were always more descriptive and interesting, and it took him a long time to tell them. The stories also had a lesson to them, and often, there was history, culture and geography in them as well.

I would always take him a mug of tea, stoke up the fire and wait until he was ready to begin. Sometimes I would suggest one of my favorites, but most often, he would remember his own. He would lay on his bed, propped up with his pillow. I would sit on my special stool. Often our story time would have to continue another night as he would get tired. Or sometimes, my Mom would come and get me for my bedtime. These times I will always remember. But I wish I had paid more attention to the history, culture, etc.

Often, when the stories ended, he would suddenly remember a place or an event. This was what I enjoyed so much. These stories were sometimes about *Windigo*, *Nainabush* and others. The stories told in our language were so vivid in the description. When translated to English, the description, the thread of the story, is lost.

My mother also told my sister and I stories. These were ones that our *Nokomis (Koomis)*, our father's mother, had told her. They were usually about the way she lived as young woman and were true events. Like how they had to be careful not to wander away from their home when doing their chores as the *Naadwe*, the Iroquois, would kidnap them. The events that she told us were true events. They made us be thankful that we had so much freedom to go wandering out in the woods.

The previous stories were about my childhood and where my father came from. I wish I had listened more carefully to the stories my dad and uncles told me. Those were some that I remember.

HBC Post, Lake Temagami, 1800s

HBC Post at Bear Island, July 27, 1898; postcard sent to Willie Friday
with "Best wishes from your old friend Jim Barr" on the back

Sophie Pott's cousins

My dad towing canoes; this is how they did it then

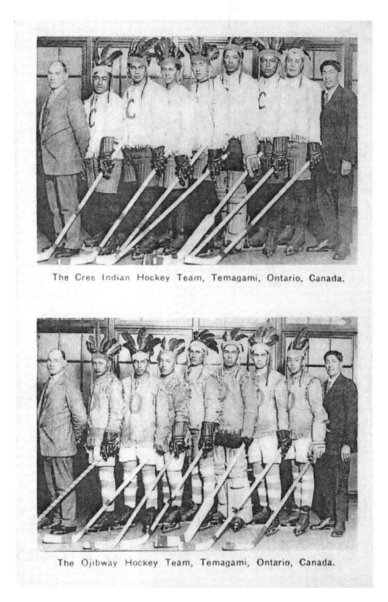

The Cree Indian Hockey Team, Temagami, Ontario, Canada.

The Ojibway Hockey Team, Temagami, Ontario, Canada.

Ojibwe and Cree hockey teams who played exhibition games
(circa 1928); far right, both pictures, Willie Friday as their manager

Grey Owl, with Doreen Saylars and Gladys, Joe Friday's daughter;
photo taken circa 1937, a year before he died

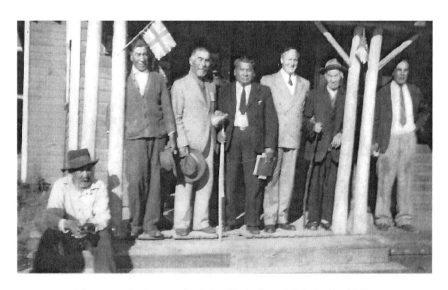

After a conference at the Friendly Indian Club in the 1940s;
standing l-r, my father, my uncle, Chief John Twain, mayor
of Bear Island, and Ontario Premier G. A. Drew

Friday's Camp lodge; standing, my mother and father

Friday's Camp lodge, view from the dock

Friday trapping cabin at Crash lake, circa 1949

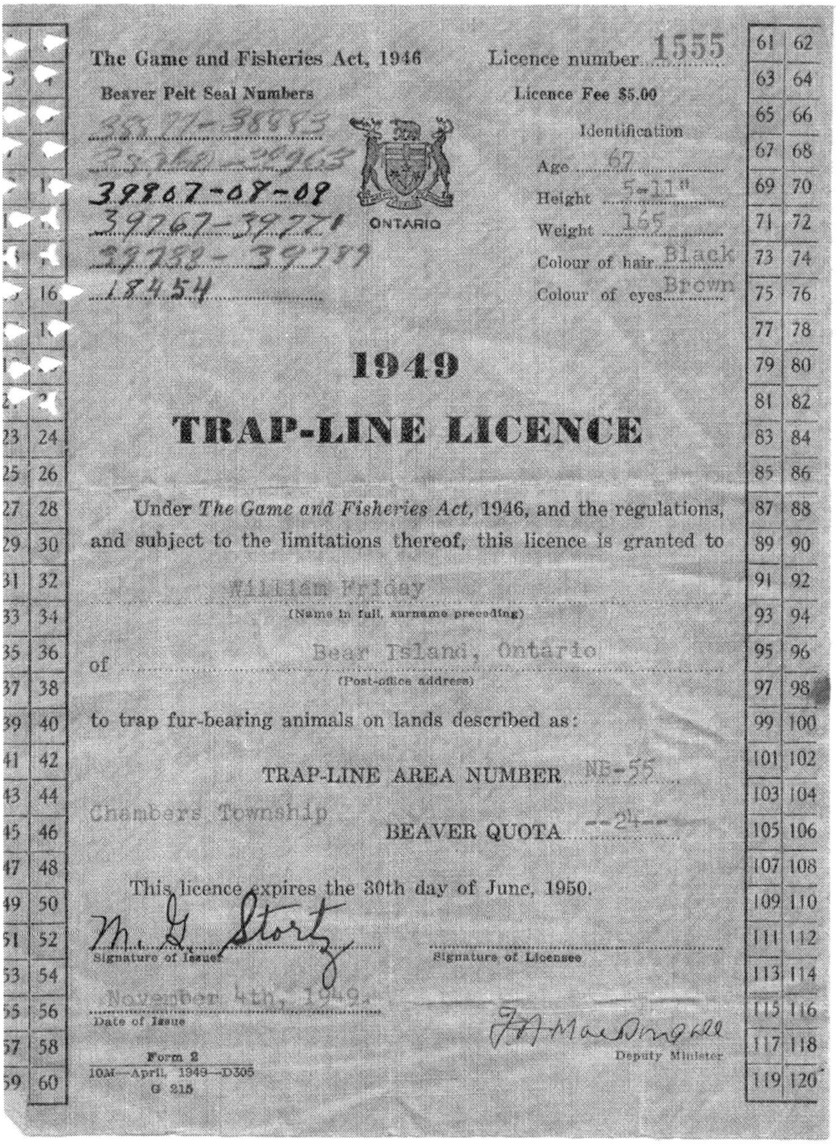
The Game and Fisheries Act, 1946

Licence number 1555

Beaver Pelt Seal Numbers

38871–38883

39760–39763

39807–08–09

39767–39771

39788–39789

18454

Licence Fee $5.00

ONTARIO

Identification

Age 67

Height 5–11"

Weight 165

Colour of hair Black

Colour of eyes Brown

1949

TRAP-LINE LICENCE

Under *The Game and Fisheries Act,* 1946, and the regulations, and subject to the limitations thereof, this licence is granted to

William Friday

(Name in full, surname preceding)

of Bear Island, Ontario

(Post-office address)

to trap fur-bearing animals on lands described as:

TRAP-LINE AREA NUMBER NB-55

Chambers Township

BEAVER QUOTA --24--

This licence expires the 30th day of June, 1950.

M. G. Stortz

Signature of Issuer

Signature of Licensee

November 4th, 1949.

Date of Issue

F.A. MacDougall

Deputy Minister

Form 2

10M—April, 1949—D305

G 215

Willie Friday's 1949 trapping licence

TRAP-LINE LICENCE

The following information is given for your convenience only:

1. — This licence is valid only within that portion of Ontario designated on the face of the licence.

2. — The licensee shall have the exclusive right to trap fur-bearing animals on Crown lands in the trap-line area designated.

3. — Where the licensee is

    (a) an owner of patented land, or a purchaser or locatee under The Public Lands Act of unpatented land in the trap-line area designated; or

    (b) the holder of a written permit from the owner, purchaser or locatee he may trap fur-bearing animals on that land.

4. — No person shall hold more than one Trap-line Licence, nor shall the holder of a Trap-line licence be the holder of a Resident Trapper's licence.

5. — The licensee shall dispose of pelts within 10 days after the expiration of the open season.

6. — The licensee shall make a true annual return of fur-bearing animals and pelts not later than July 15th, 1951, and send it to the District Forester of the district in which the licence was issued.

SEASONS

Only as provided by Regulations.

ROYALTIES

The royalties for taking or shipping to any point outside Ontario, fur-bearing animals or their pelts or sending any of them to a tanner or taxidermist to be tanned or plucked or treated in any way shall be as follows:

Beaver	$2.00	Marten	$1.00
Fisher	1.50	Mink	.50
Fox (cross)	.50	Muskrat	.10
Fox (red)	.10	Otter	1.00
Fox (silver, black or blue)	.50	Raccoon	.10
Fox (white)	.50	Skunk	.05
Fox (not specified)	.50	Weasel (ermine)	.05
Lynx	1.50	Wolverine	.40

IMPORTANT

As the licensee of this trap-line area, your efforts in keeping trails and portages open and your assistance in helping to fight any fire which may occur on the area, will be most valuable.

Back of Willie Friday's 1950 trapping licence

At Joe Friday's funeral, 1955; back l-r Donald Potts, Jim Friday, Phil Potts and John; front l-r Louie Leduc, Hazel Cannen, Sophie Potts-Friday, Annie Leduc

At Friday's Point

Part 3
A Family of my Own

My son Rick's baptism; front l-r my parents with my niece
Louise and her father (my brother) behind them,
then Bishop Wright and me holding Rick

When my son Rick was about six or seven years old, we were living in the old house on Mill Street in Callander. We had taken him to see Peter Pan with Mary Martin. When we got home, I was making a snack in the kitchen and Rick was around the corner in the living room and talking about the movie, and Dad (my husband Don) was fiddling with the black and white TV. Rick decided he was Peter Pan and jumped off the back of the couch thinking he could fly. Down he went! I'll always remember that!

Friday's lodge veranda, spring 1955;
l-r Gary Potts, Verna Friday, Linda Potts, and Tom and Louise Friday
(Verna's siblings, my brother's children); in front on his tricycle, my son Rick

When Robert was in grade one, Grandma Friday was staying with us. She always got Robert ready for bed. After he was washed up, he would read to Grandma. She always had a glass of water beside her bed at night. He would also want one. This habit, he kept up till his teens.

When he was eighteen months old or so, he was always climbing up on the counter and digging in the kitchen cupboards. He got his arm in the wringer washer once while Grandma and I were doing laundry.

Don had to put up a snow fence around three sides of the house so that Robert and Donnie wouldn't get out on Mill Street.

One time, Robert was pulling on toys, and then on the whole toy box, and over they went. Loose on the go! Don pulled it down that night. Another time, we couldn't find him in his bunk bed. We searched the whole house. No Robert. We woke Rick up. He didn't know where he was. Then finally, we looked under the bed and there he was, sound asleep.

When my boys were young, my husband and I took our holidays camping at Lady Evelyn, Diamond Lake and Crash Lake, where my dad's trapping area was. Crash Lake has a different name now. The trapping grounds are now trapped by my nephew, a Friday. My husband and our oldest son went moose hunting where my dad's trapping grounds are. One time, we hiked into the bush and lo and behold, there was this logging road and a huge truck that came roaring down upon us. The truck stopped and one man who could speak English told us they were from Quebec and that they had killed all the moose in that area.

So back to the cabin we went, and my husband decided to go get the other boys, the dog and more food and make a holiday for all of us. Those trips that we spent together we'll always remember. This was in the fall, but we also went on fishing trips there. They were fun. Listening on a cold moon-lit night to the wolves howling, telling each other of our arrival. Also hearing fox barking and rabbits whistling. The boys had set rabbit snares, but Old Red Fox got to the snares first! That's when they realized they had to get up really early to go check their snares.

My husband and I often went for a paddle in a canoe. This was in the spring, when we went down to Spawning Bay or as my nieces and nephews called it, Grandma's Narrows. One time, as we were nearing the portage, there was a mother bear and her three cubs at the water's edge. When the mother bear heard and saw us, she grunted, calling her babies to run after her into the bush. But one little cub didn't listen. The cub stopped and was looking back at us. Mother bear called again, but he didn't listen, so mama bear came back and got behind the cub and with her paw, she slapped his behind, like you would do to a child, only the little bear went flying in the air so high, I thought it was a goner. But then when he landed the cub took off really fast, with mamma bear right behind. That was quite a scene and I never saw that happen again.

At that same spot, my husband and I walked on the ice to go and see what fish we had in a net. This narrows stays open all winter and it was where my mother set her fish net. We were getting the canoe down from where it was hung up in a tree, so that animals wouldn't wreck it. Suddenly, my husband pointed across the open water, where a huge rock went into the lake. There were three otters. They would slide down the rock on their back into the water. Then back up they would go, and down again. We just sat and watched for half an hour or more. Finally, they swam off.

Grandma's Narrows was a very special place for me and my family. In the spring, when the lake was clear of ice, the pickerel season opened. We fished there, along with other people in their boats. Sometimes I counted twenty boats. What fun we had visiting, catching fish and comparing who caught the largest and the most. There is no more fishing at that spot anymore, but good times were had there.

Me in younger days

Souvenir of the Li'l Beavers of Ontario Summer Days, July 17-21 1978,
l-r me, another June and Mrs Stevens

My husband Don with baby Crystal

Part 4
Life on My Own

I'll fast-forward to when I became a widow. I changed my life. I was working, but I wanted to be "me", as people thought of me as 'Don's widow'. A dear friend, whom I knew for many years, suggested that since I spoke my language, why not go to Lakehead University to learn how to teach it? She got me all the information and application forms. I arranged my holidays for one month and sent my tape and application in, and hoped that I would be accepted. I was accepted and what an experience I had for three years.

As an Ojibwe teacher with other teachers; there I am, sitting in the middle

When I was with the Friendship Centre, going to assemblies, I would go to where the Elders would be teaching about culture, native spirituality and medicine. I became involved in my community with Moon ceremonies, anything that would benefit my beliefs. I was now finding a new way of life and belief for myself.

At that time, we had a respected Elder in the community working as the tenants' counsellor for the Native Housing for Seniors where I lived. I had many questions about ceremonies, culture… and "what about sweats?" He gave me so much information. I was thinking of going traditional and leaving my church.

One Easter Sunday, along with my son, his wife and my grandchildren, we went to our Easter services. As I was at the altar, receiving Holy Communion, I heard a voice say: "Go for a sweat." I glanced at my son, next to me, but he was looking at the altar. When we got back to our pew, I asked him if he said to me "Go for a sweat." He said "No, we don't talk at the altar when we go for communion." I heard the voice say that three times. When Monday came, I rushed down to the office and told the Elder what happened to me. He said: "I guess you'd better go for a sweat." So I gave him tobacco and went to my first sweat. I was now on my path to a traditional way.

I did try to combine my religion and the traditional path, but it didn't work for me. Some people can combine both and be quite happy and content. After that, I attended pow wows and ceremonies, any kind I was invited to attend.

Then, nine or ten years ago, my cousin invited me to attend a weekend workshop at the Wellness Clinic at Bear Island. There were two facilitators who were traditional Elders. In the three days, I absorbed and learned so much. It was then that I knew that's what I wanted and where I belonged, and that I had so much more to learn. Isabelle and Caroline (the Elders) took me under their wings and became my mentors. From then on, I attended many, many ceremonies. I was also teaching my language at Bear Island on weekends, and so many wonderful, exciting things happened to me once I embraced my native culture and traditions. I have had so many exciting experiences and met many, many wonderful traditional people who have helped me on my journey.

Many friends told me that I should keep a journal. I have tried, but never seem to remember to write in it. I guess this is my journal, these stories, memories that I write about. At my age, I now sit and relive the things that have happened years ago and write about them.

One of my mentors, Caroline, gave me books to read, and the author was Lynn Andrews. I thought the stories were fiction, and I asked Caroline about the author and her stories. She said the author was alive and the stories were true. She also told me Lynn Andrews held workshops in New York, Los Angeles and New Mexico and that she was going to New Mexico as it was cheaper than the others. I asked if I could go with her as I wanted to meet the lady who wrote about Native culture and spiritual things that happened to her. So off I went to Albuquerque, New Mexico for five days.

The climate there is so different and the scenery so very different from northern Ontario. The ranch was run by Mexicans who couldn't figure out who Caroline and I were. We were the only Natives on the ranch among about two hundred and fifty people. The group I was with had about twenty women of different ages. I was the eldest and they treated me with the respect that Native people show towards their Elders.

I really enjoyed the workshops and teachings. The teachings were given by Lynn Andrews herself. I absorbed as much as I could and on our last day, I got her to autograph her book. She shook hands with me and told me, without my saying anything about myself to her, that I was on the right path and that I had two good mentors like she had in her books. I was so overjoyed and thrilled. I still think about it, as it gives me a good feeling. That trip I shall never, ever forget!

Part 5
In Memory of my Daughter

August 2005

Thursday, August 18th: *Ron and Jessie arrived amidst the drizzling rain. I went down to the boat and saw Melissa's headstone and sat awhile with her urn. I hope the weather clears up for Saturday.*

Friday, August 19th: *Ron, Tom, Rob and I drove to the graveyard with the headstone and selected a place above Doug's grave. It is hard digging, lots of rocks! The stone is put in place and a hole is dug for the urn. Rain and more rain.*

Shawna and I cleaned up at Rick's for tomorrow. We'll mix my salad tomorrow!

Saturday, August 20th: *Misty day, but warm. I hope and pray that it clears up! Tom and Johnny are getting sand to use to fill in the hole. Everyone arrived at 1:15, 1:30 or so. Waiting on Rick, Raphael, Evan, Nancy, Crystal, Shawna, Johnnie, Rob and Barb, Don and Linda, Diane, Tom, Jenny, Eric, Ron, Jessie, Verna, Steve and me. (20) We all arrive over in Ron's boat, with Johnnie, Rob and Steve. I arrived last. I smudged and explained why and did those who wanted to. Did her urn* *and stone and hole. Evan read the verse in her funeral notice. It said it all, how we felt! Asked if anyone wanted to say anything. Asked Jessie and Jen to put flowers down and Barb added a wee tree. We all put sand in. Ron first, and so on. Now she is with the Fridays!*

Back to Rick's for a huge meal. Fresh fish, beans, salad, etc. Rain sprinkle. Fire outside, feels good. My sons, Ron, Linda, Raphael all say that I did well. It was the Creator who guided me and gave me the right words and strength!

Sunday, August 21st: *Home, and I feel at peace. Now it is final but she will never be forgotten.*

Melissa, doing what she loved to do

The Moose Hunt

Story told by June and recorded in North Bay, on March 30, 2013

I went up there (to my daughter's home) *because she was going to school and her partner was working so I went up there to go and babysit 'cause they were going to go moose hunting. They were taking time off. So anyway, they left. (Laughs) So that morning I got the girls and they went to school and I tidied up in the house and then at about nine thirty, quarter to ten, in they popped! And I said: "What's the matter?" and Ron came limping in and headed for the couch - he'd put his back out. He had a bad back. So she was kind of disgusted because she had taken time off from school just for that… 'Cause she was doing two things, working at Wal-Mart and going to school.*

So you understand, she was kind of mad and he said "Why don't you take your mother?" "Me?" I said, "I can't moose hunt, I don't have a gun licence." (Laughs) "No, no" he said, "you'll be the watcher." I said "What does a watcher do?" "Well, what do you think: watch for moose."

So I said "All right, I'll go". So I told her "I have to go home and get clothes, warm clothes." 'Cause you know, you need to dress warm, this was November, latter part of October, early part of November. So I came home and I got some warm clothes. We went to bed early. We got up at four, and away she and I went. She loaded her guns in the car, and we stopped at Tim Horton's to get coffee and away we went.

This was around four thirty in the morning and, surprisingly (laughs) I said what are all those guys doing in Tim Horton's and she said "What do you think; they're going moose hunting too." "But," she said, "we're early."

So we stopped at this one field and she got out of the car, and she started calling moose. And I was looking at her: "I never even knew you could do that." "Yeah," she said "…listen, see if you hear any answers…" But we didn't hear anything, so I said, "How far more?" It was just starting to get daylight. And she said "Well, we'll go up this road," which was an old lumber road. (We were in Quebec, way past that Deux-rivières, on—what do you call it—the government grounds.)

So anyway, I said, "Have you got your guns ready?" and she said "Yeah I guess I better get them out of there." So she got them out of the trunk, unwrapped them and put them on the back seat. "Now," I said (laughs), "what do I do?" "Well," she said, "we're going up this road and I want you to watch, see if you see any moose."

And we go around this bend, oh that was beautiful, we're just going around the bend and on my right-hand side was this great big hill with pines and small hardwood, beautiful, and the sun shining on it eh, and I said "Look-it! There's one!" and she stopped and said "There's two! That looks like a cow and a calf!" So she drove up a little further and we got out.

And oh I was just shaking; you'd think I was the one that was the hunter. And she got out, and she had her gun on top of the roof eh. She turned and oh this is funny, she turned to me, and said "Which one should I shoot first Mom?" "You're the hunter, not me!" I said, "I don't know!" She said: "Well, maybe I should shoot the calf first and get the cow later, you know 'cause the calf will run away."

Anyway she took the shot and away it went, and away she went and left me there. So anyway, away she went chasing after them and she did get one, she got the calf and she chased after the cow, she was going after the cow then, and I could hear a shot and another shot and the next thing I heard was the bush cracking! I jumped back in the car, it was only about a hundred feet ahead of me eh, like there's another bend in the road, and I'm sitting there, thinking "Oh my god, now what."

So, she comes walking out of the bush, and says "Did she come down this way?" And I said "Yeah, there's something in the bush over there".

"Yeah," she said "you know what happened... Oh, I'll tell you later!" So away she went in front of me, and I walked behind her, and here's this great big, oh my god it looked huge, it looked as high as a telephone pole. And it was the cow moose, a great big... and it was standing on its hind legs, you know, she had injured her. And I said "Don't you think you should shoot it again?" "No," she said, "I gave her a lung shot. I hit her in the lungs." And I said "Are you sure?" "Yea-ah," she said.

So anyway, all of a sudden it collapsed. So she said "I'll go see if it's dead." I said "Make sure you're gun's cocked cause your grandpa used to say, sometimes they play possum too eh." So she went up to it and she poked it and it was dead.

So now, she said, "Now we've got to go back and tell Ron. Cause I have to get the four-wheeler, and then get a branch and start brushing the blood, and you know, the tracks." And I said "What are we doing this for?', and she said "What do you think, somebody might come along and take my moose, see the blood, the size of it eh." And so we did that. So anyway, we got back, we drove back. It must have been about 11 o'clock in the morning by the time we got back to the house. Ron was laying on the couch.

Oh I was so excited. I went in the door, and he says "Well?" I said "We got two!" "Two? Holy jeez!" he says. You know, all that work eh. Then she came in behind me and he said "Why did you shoot two for?" So she said "I had to." (Laughs) So anyway, they started on the phone while I stayed there. Well, it was eight o'clock that night, before he got two friends with the four-wheelers and trailers, and made arrangements to hang the moose. Yeah, they got them hung up and then they had to fix them...

So what had happened was when she chased after that moose, ha, she walked right into a yard... a moose yard! (Laughs) There was a whole bunch of moose laying there! (Laughs) But she was after this one eh. (Recorder: She could have just walked in there and picked one out!) Yeah, *exactly, (laughs) but she was after that cow, that's what she had a licence for eh.*

Oh my I was never so excited, I couldn't get over that, all that, oh... that was ... and oh, I was so... Ron laughed at me. He said "What are you so excited and shaken about?" And I said "That's the first time I've ever done that!" And it was. I had gone years ago with my dad, but I was just a kid, and I got scared. (Laughs) When we were in the canoe I could hear the moose coming, my dad was calling eh, the canoe was up on the shore, and I started crying (laughs) and scared the moose away. So they never took me again. (Laughs) I don't blame them, eh.

You know, she was quite the hunter. She shot those two moose, and then the following weekend or two weekends later she went to Calgary with Ron, it was deer season, the deer season was open eh, and she shot a deer down there. It's so funny, cause Rick, Robert and Don, they hunted partridge, but they weren't moose hunters or deer hunters, and here she was, she just loved that, you know, she just lived to go hunting and fishing. That was the best time I ever had... that's one memory I have of her.

June Friday MacInnis, at home in North Bay, Ont., fall 2015

Biography

I was born on June 11, 1931 at home, at Friday's Point on Lake Temagami, in northeastern Ontario. I attended school at home and in North Bay. I also attended Lakehead University in Thunder Bay, from which I graduated as an Ojibwe language teacher. I was married and lived in Callander for forty-four years on the same street. I have three sons and had a daughter who died of cancer. I have six lovely granddaughters, one beautiful grandson and six precious great-grand-sons. While I lived in Callander, I did a lot of volunteering with local political council elections. I was involved with the North Bay Indian Friendship Centre as a board member and in many positions, and also with the board of the Ontario Federation of Indian Friendship Centers for a time.

I also served on the Children's Aid board as Native representative for nine years. And I travelled to my reserve and taught the language at adult workshops. I've had two mentors who became my good friends and instructed me about the culture and spiritual values, which I am proud to carry as an Ojibwe grandmother. At present (2015) I am president of our Native People of Nipissing Non-Profit Housing Corporation and have been for the past 38 years.

CPSIA information can be obtained at www.ICGtesting.com
Printed in the USA
LVOW10*2319230616

493879LV00002B/9/P